Contents

What is a wetland?   4

Where are the wetlands?   6

What plants grow in wet places?   8

Does Africa have wetlands?   10

Are hippos dangerous?   13

What is a delta?   14

Are all wetlands big?   16

What's the biggest wetland?   18

Is the Amazon rainforest a wetland?   20

What's below the surface?   23

What other scary creatures live in wetlands?   24

Do people live in wetlands?   26

Are wetlands in danger?   28

Wetland facts   30

Glossary   31

Index   32

Painted terrapin

Swordtail

Electric eel

What is a wetland?

A wetland is just that: land that is swampy and wet for all or part of the time. Oceans, seas, rivers and big lakes are not wetlands. Wetlands occur all over the world, in warm regions and cold. In this book you'll meet a few of the creatures and plants that live in wetlands – and some of them are really scary!

Everything shown here lives in a wetland, though not all in the same one! The animals are not all drawn to the same scale.

African pygmy goose

Nile crocodile

Blister beetle

Waterlilies

Hippopotamus

Jewelled cichlid

Scary Creatures
of the
WETLANDS

Written by
Penny Clarke

BOOK HOUSE

Created and designed
by David Salariya

Author:

Penny Clarke is an author and editor
specialising in information books for children. She has
written books on natural history, rainforests and
volcanoes, as well as others on different periods of
history. She used to live in central London, but thanks
to modern technology she has now realised her dream
of being able to live and work in the countryside.

Artists:

John Francis

Mark Bergin

Carolyn Scrace

Li Sidong

Julian Baker

Series Creator:

David Salariya was born in Dundee,
Scotland. He established The Salariya Book Company
in 1989. He has illustrated a wide range of books and
has created many new series for publishers in the UK
and overseas. He lives in Brighton with his wife,
illustrator Shirley Willis, and their son.

Editors: Tanya Kant, Stephen Haynes

Editorial Assistant: Rob Walker

Picture Research:
Mark Bergin, Carolyn Franklin

Photo Credits:

t=top, m=middle, b=bottom

Mark Bergin: 29
Dreamstime: 15t, 19m, 19b, 23, 25t
Fotolia: 6–7, 13, 14, 15b, 18, 19
Carolyn Franklin: 25b
Mountain High Maps/© 1993 Digital
  Wisdom Inc.: 6–7
Photodisc: 10, 28
Topfoto: 26, 27t
U.S. Army Corps of Engineers: 27b

Great diving beetle

Published in Great Britain in 2008 by
Book House, an imprint of
The Salariya Book Company Ltd
25 Marlborough Place, Brighton BN1 1UB

SALARIYA

A catalogue record for this book is available
from the British Library.

HB ISBN: 978-1-906370-52-7
PB ISBN: 978-1-906370-53-4

Printed in China

PAPER FROM
SUSTAINABLE
FORESTS

Visit our website at **www.salariya.com**
for *free* electronic versions of:
You Wouldn't Want to be an Egyptian Mummy!
You Wouldn't Want to be a Roman Gladiator!
Avoid Joining Shackleton's Polar Expedition!
Avoid Sailing on a 19th-Century Whaling Ship!

Wetlands can be made up of fresh, **brackish** or salty water. Most living things have evolved to live in only one kind of wetland.

African fish eagle

Yellow bittern

Sitatunga

African jacana

Malachite kingfisher

Otters

Purple heron

Dragonfly

Dwarf mouth-brooder

Pirate butterfly

Emerald tree frog

Tigerfish

African pike

Where are the wetlands?

There are wetlands on every continent except Antarctica. Rivers are not wetlands, but wetlands often form beside rivers. Each year, for example, the rivers Nile and Amazon flood huge areas along their banks, forming wetlands. Until these areas dry up, they are home to huge numbers of insects, birds, **amphibians** and creatures that prey on them.

The alligator snapping turtle lives in the Everglades wetland in Florida, USA. It has a pink, wormlike 'lure' in its mouth. When it lurks in slow-running water with its mouth open, fish are easy **prey**.

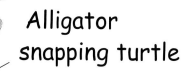

Alligator snapping turtle

Frogs, toads and newts are amphibians. They have lungs, breathe air and live on land, but lay their eggs in water.

North America

Everglades

Tropic of Cancer

Central America

Equator

Amazon basin

Tropic of Capricorn

South America

Major wetland areas

Mangroves

Mangrove trees form swamps around coasts in **tropical** regions. Their tangled **aerial roots** trap **silt** and vegetation.

Marbled newt

Willow tree

Newts live in **temperate** wetlands all over the world.

Arctic wetlands

Europe

Asia

Africa

Nile valley and delta

Australasia

Antarctica

Trees such as willows grow well in wet or waterlogged ground.

European green toad

Green toads go to wetlands to breed. The females can lay two strings of eggs, with up to 20,000 eggs in each string.

The world's largest wetland forms each summer in the **Arctic** regions of the northern **hemisphere**. As the long winter ends, the frozen ground thaws to form a huge swamp.

What plants grow in wet places?

Most plants rot in wet soil, but some have evolved so they don't. Reeds grow through shallow water near the bank, waterlilies float on the surface, and a few plants, like the Canadian pondweed, grow underwater. To grow, plants must absorb water and **nutrients** through their roots. Swampy soil has few nutrients, so some plants, like the pitcher plant, have found surprising ways to survive.

Most of these plants and animals live in the damp areas at the edges of ponds, lakes and streams. Big pike lurk in the shadow of the reeds waiting for their prey.

Waterlily

Frogs

Pike

Did you know?

The world's largest waterlily grows in the **sluggish** backwaters of the River Amazon. The leaves of the royal waterlily (*Victoria amazonica*) can be more than 2 metres across.

Pitcher plant

Fly

Lip of
pitcher

Cutaway
view of the
'pitcher'

Some plants survive by eating insects! As its name suggests, the pitcher plant has a deep pouch like a pitcher, or jar. This contains liquid chemicals which attract flies. The flies land on the slippery lip of the pitcher and fall into the liquid. The plant then digests the flies and absorbs the nutrients it needs.

Yellow
cress

Water
crowfoot

Butterbur

Many wetland plants don't rot because they grow in places that are not wet all the time. Plants like butterbur, cress and crowfoot grow in cooler climates. They grow best when the ground is wet, but can survive when it is only damp. Even when wetlands dry out, some plants can still survive as seeds.

Does Africa have wetlands?

Africa has **seasonal** wetlands which form in the rainy season and dry up in the summer heat. These wetlands are vital for Africa's wildlife. The River Nile, the world's longest river, flows 6,695 km from central Africa north to the Mediterranean Sea. Vast areas of wetland exist on the Nile's banks, as well as on those of the Congo River in central Africa.

X-Ray Vision

Hold the next page up to the light to see the hippo's skull.

See what's inside

Elephants and baboons by a river that is shrinking in Africa's summer heat

Hippos live in African wetlands. They spend much of their time in shallow rivers, lakes or swamps. They are **herbivores** – they eat plants – but that doesn't mean they are friendly!

Turn the page to learn more about these scary creatures.

'Hippo' is short for 'hippopotamus', which means 'river horse' in Greek.

Eye socket

Upper canine teeth

Tusks (lower canine teeth)

Powerful jawbone

The hippo's 'tusks' are really very large **canine teeth**.

Are hippos dangerous?

Yes, even though they are herbivores! Hippos live in groups, and the males fight to be leader of their group and to claim territory on the riverbank. They will also attack people in the water, and even small boats. Hippos may look clumsy, but they swim and dive well, helped by the four webbed toes on each foot.

Did you know?

When hippos swim underwater, they close their nostrils to keep the water out.

Hippos eat so much vegetation that they keep wetland edges clear of plants. This allows other animals to get to the water.

Fights between male hippos often cause bad injuries, but rarely death.

What is a delta?

Great rivers carry huge quantities of fine soil, called silt. As the river approaches the sea, the water flows more slowly and the silt sinks to the bottom. Over thousands of years this silt builds up to form an area of low-lying land called a **delta**. Deltas are **fertile** places, so there is plenty of food and water. They can be good places for humans and wildlife to live, but there is always a danger of floods.

This delta land is only a little higher than the river, so flooding is a constant danger – and **global warming** could make the danger even worse.

Wetland predator

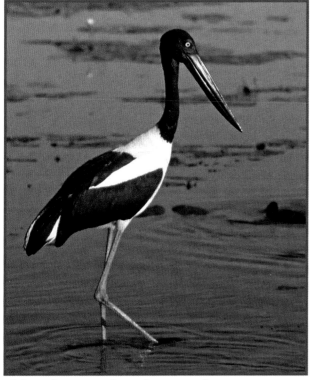

Black-necked stork

The black-necked stork lives in the wetlands of Asia and Australasia. Its long legs help it to wade through the water as it creeps towards its prey. With its long neck and beak it stabs forward, catching its prey by surprise.

When a river flows through low-lying land it often forms wide curves known as meanders. When the river floods it may break its banks and flow straight across. Then the meanders are cut off to form U-shaped 'oxbow' lakes.

Meanders

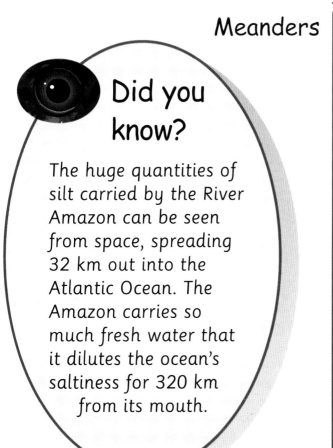

Did you know?

The huge quantities of silt carried by the River Amazon can be seen from space, spreading 32 km out into the Atlantic Ocean. The Amazon carries so much fresh water that it dilutes the ocean's saltiness for 320 km from its mouth.

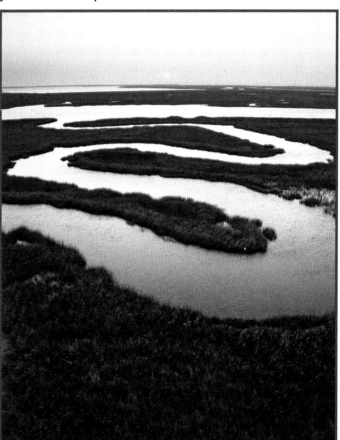

Bromeliad

Wetlands aren't always on the ground! In rainforest trees, pools of water create miniature wetlands where tiny frogs and insects live and breed.

Are all wetlands big?

No, but fearsome creatures live even in small ones! Most frogs and toads lay their eggs at the edges of wetlands. The eggs hatch into tadpoles – vicious hunters of tiny insects and fish **larvae**. But other hunters lie in wait for the tadpoles.

The dragonfly nymph is an early stage in the life cycle of the dragonfly. It lurks in shallow water, grabbing tadpoles in its strong jaws. Diving beetles also feed on tadpoles. That's why frogs and toads have to lay so many eggs.

Cranefly

Dragonfly nymph

Tadpoles

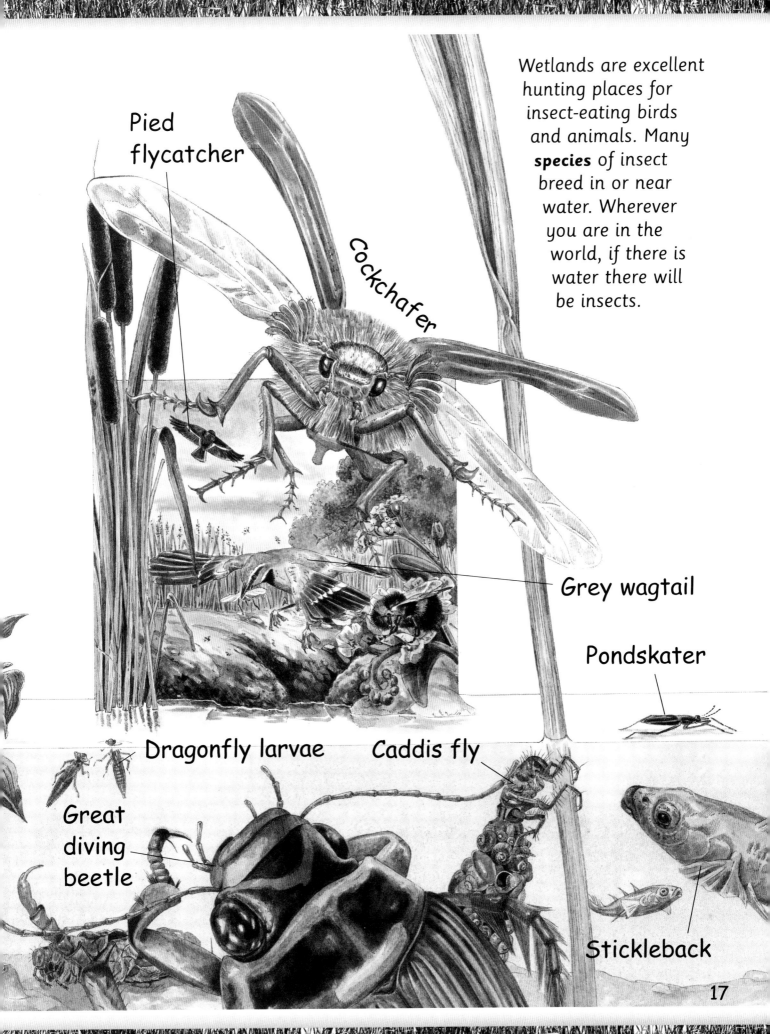

Pied
flycatcher

Cockchafer

Wetlands are excellent
hunting places for
insect-eating birds
and animals. Many
species of insect
breed in or near
water. Wherever
you are in the
world, if there is
water there will
be insects.

Grey wagtail

Pondskater

Dragonfly larvae

Caddis fly

Great
diving
beetle

Stickleback

What's the biggest wetland?

The world's largest wetland is also one of its coldest regions: the **tundra** of northern Europe and Asia. During the long Arctic winter the land is frozen hard; but in summer the top few centimetres of land thaw. The water cannot drain away because the ground below remains frozen, so the tundra becomes a huge bog. Insects breed in millions, then birds arrive to feed on them and to breed. In turn, the large number of birds attracts many other **predators**.

A lone polar bear on the frozen winter tundra

Arctic fox in summer

Most birds fly south as the Arctic winter sets in, but some birds and mammals stay. To help them survive in the snow-covered land, the ptarmigan and Arctic fox lose their summer colours and turn white. This gives **camouflage** for both hunter (the Arctic fox) and hunted (the ptarmigan).

Male ptarmigan changing to winter colours

Polar bears (opposite page) are among the world's scariest creatures, but they live in the Arctic where there are few people. These dangerous bears can outrun humans, and stand 3 metres tall when they rear up on their hind legs.

Did you know?

'Reindeer' and 'caribou' are different names for the same animal. The caribou of North America is the reindeer of northern Europe. Both males and females have antlers – they are the only deer in the world to do so.

Reindeer/ caribou

X-Ray Vision

Hold the next page up to the light to see what's happening beneath the suface.

See what's inside

Alligator

Giant armadillo

The thick vegetation on the Amazon's banks provides **habitats** for many creatures, from huge snakes to tiny insects.

Is the Amazon rainforest a wetland?

Yes. Each year, from January to August, the River Amazon rises up to 9 metres and floods vast areas of forest on its banks. Without the fertile silt the flood leaves behind, the forest could not grow. And without lush vegetation there would be none of this colourful wildlife.

Anaconda

Snakes are among the forest's scariest hunters. Their jaws expand so they can swallow prey bigger than their heads.

Hoatzin

Green-winged
macaws

Caiman

Hyacinth macaw

Capybara

Anaconda

Collared peccary

Electric eel

Catfish

Caiman

Piranhas

Capybara

What's below the surface?

Tapir

This rainforest pool is teeming with predators and prey. Capybaras are related to guinea pigs. They can grow to 1.3 metres and are excellent swimmers, but that doesn't help them when there's a hungry alligator or caiman nearby. Attracted by the smell of blood, piranhas quickly appear. On the bank an anaconda tackles a peccary (a wild pig). It coils its muscular body around the animal, then it contracts its muscles, crushing the prey to death.

Brazilian tapirs live in swampy forests, sleeping by day and eating plants at night. Although they can grow up to 2 metres long, they are hunted by anacondas and boas – snakes that kill by crushing their prey. After a tapir meal, the snake need not eat for months!

What other scary creatures live in wetlands?

One of the smallest and deadliest wetland creatures is the mosquito. Mosquitoes carry diseases that can kill humans, such as malaria, yellow fever and dengue fever. For thousands of years no-one understood the link between mosquitoes and these diseases – but people knew that wetlands could be unhealthy places.

Did you know?

In the 1880s, thousands of men building the Panama Canal died of malaria.

Catfish

Piranhas

Rosy tetra

Discus fish

Catfish use their 'whiskers' or barbels to search for food in muddy water.

Electric eels really do electrocute their prey. They have special organs that can produce up to 500 volts of electricity. This isn't likely to kill a healthy human, but you'd get a very nasty shock.

Electric organs

Electric eel

Burmese python

Burmese pythons now live in Florida's Everglades. Originally imported as pets, they escaped or were let loose by their owners. They have made themselves at home and are now a threat to people and pets.

The estuarine crocodile of south-east Asia and Australia can be 6 metres long. It kills its prey – sometimes including humans – by dragging it underwater.

Estuarine crocodile

Do people live in wetlands?

Perhaps the best-known people living in wetlands today are the Madan or Marsh Arabs of southern Iraq. They live in the area of the Tigris and Euphrates rivers. The vast marshes between these two great rivers were drained and burnt by the then Iraqi government in the 1990s, but now the marshes are being restored.

It will take time for the marshes to recover, but already the people have started to return – and so have birds and fish.

Building in reed

The tall columns at the front of this Marsh Arab house are made from bundles of reeds.

The traditional *mudhif* or village meeting house of the Marsh Arabs is made entirely of reeds. Even the foundations are made of reeds packed down hard and covered with mud from the marshes. No other building materials are available here.

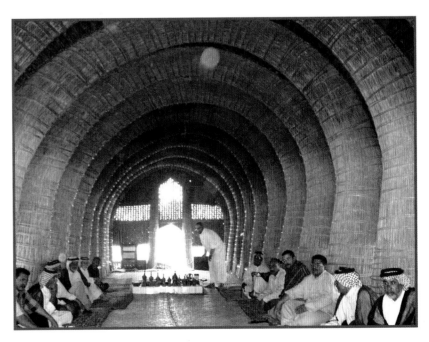

Inside an Iraqi mudhif

Are wetlands in danger?

Sadly, many wetlands are in danger. As the world's population increases, wetlands are drained to create more land for homes. This destroys the habitats of many plants and animals. Drained land shrinks, and if it is below sea level it will flood. If the land is flooded with salt water, it may be years before crops can grow there again.

Wetlands are often drained to make space for power stations or rubbish dumps. The damage caused by pollution like this will last longer than anyone alive today. Perhaps human beings are the scariest creatures of all!

Tourists in Florida

Tourism can damage wetlands, but it can also help people to realise how beautiful and important they are. In the Florida Everglades, slow-moving boats take visitors through the waterways where they can see animals such as alligators (below) without harming them.

Did you know?

Wetlands around the Mediterranean Sea are essential stopovers for birds migrating between Europe and Africa.

Wetland facts

Many wetland areas are covered with water plants. Birds called jacanas (see page 5) have very long toes that allow them to walk over the plants as they hunt insects, seeds and snails.

There are many reports of estuarine crocodiles hunting humans in the swamps of northern Australia. Climbing a tree is not the answer – the crocs will lie in wait close by.

In mangrove swamps from east Africa to Australia, fish called mudskippers live up to their name. They move briskly over muddy ground and climb mangrove roots to bask in the sun.

The ancient Egyptians owed their prosperity to the River Nile. The Nile floods each year. The silt left on the land by the flood makes it very fertile, so crops grow well there.

Small seasonal wetlands, especially in hot African climates, are in great danger if the annual rains fail. As the land dries up, the vegetation dies. If the **drought** lasts several years, the trees may never regrow.

In temperate regions, if the climate becomes drier a wetland may become a woodland. First coarse grass moves in, then small shrubs. Larger shrubs follow, then trees take over.

The South African rain frog and bullfrog live in seasonal wetlands. They spend the dry periods underground and come to the surface only when it rains. Then they breed and feed. As the land dries out, they burrow deep into the ground again.

The huge leaves of the Amazon's royal waterlily have air-filled ribs that help them float.

Crocodiles and alligators can replace their worn teeth. They grow new, sharp teeth that push the old ones out.

Much of the land in Bangladesh is below sea level. This sometimes causes disastrous floods.

Royal waterlily

Glossary

aerial roots Roots that are partly above ground.

amphibian A **cold-blooded** animal that can live on land or in water, but breeds only in water.

Arctic The part of the Earth north of the Arctic Circle (latitude 66° 33' north of the Equator).

brackish Slightly salty (referring to water).

bromeliad A type of plant with fleshy leaves, which often lives on other plants.

camouflage Markings or colouring on a creature that help it blend in with its surroundings.

canine tooth A pointed tooth for tearing food.

cold-blooded Having a body temperature that changes with the temperature of the air.

delta A triangular area of land formed from silt deposited at a river's mouth.

drought A lack of rainfall.

Equator The imaginary line around the centre of the Earth, dividing the two hemispheres.

fertile Rich in nutrients.

global warming A gradual rise in the temperature of the Earth's atmosphere, partly caused by carbon dioxide and other polluting emissions.

habitat The place where a plant or animal lives naturally.

hemispheres The two halves of the Earth, north and south of the Equator.

herbivore An animal that eats only plants.

larva (plural **larvae**) A young animal that will change into a different form when it becomes an adult.

nutrient Anything that gives nourishment.

predator Any animal that kills other animals for food.

prey Any animal that is killed by another animal for food.

seasonal Changing with the seasons.

silt Very fine soil carried by rivers.

sluggish Slow-moving.

species A group of plants or animals that look alike, live in the same way and produce young that do the same.

temperate Neither very hot nor very cold.

tropical Belonging to the tropics – the part of the Earth that lies between the Tropics of Cancer and Capricorn (see pages 6–7). This area has the warmest climate on Earth.

tundra The Arctic region where the soil below the surface never thaws.

Index

A

Africa 10–11
alligator 20, 23, 29
Amazon 6, 8, 15, 20–23
amphibians 6–7
Arctic 7, 18–19
armadillo 20

B

baboon 10
birds 4, 5, 15, 17, 19, 20, 21
bromeliad 16

C

caiman 21–23
camouflage 19
canine teeth 12
capybara 21–23
caribou 19
Congo River 10
crocodile 25

D

delta 14
disease 24
draining of wetlands 26, 28

E

electric eel 3, 22, 24
elephant 10
Everglades, Florida 6, 25, 29

F

fish 3, 4, 5, 8, 17, 22–24, 30
fox 19
frog 5, 8, 16

G

global warming 14

H

herbivores 11, 13
hippopotamus 4, 11–13
humans 13, 19, 25, 28

I

insects 2, 4, 5, 9, 16, 17, 18, 24

L

larvae 16, 17

M

Madan 26–27
mangrove 6–7
map 6–7
Marsh Arabs 26–27
meanders 15
mudhif 27

N

newt 6–7
Nile 6, 7, 10
nutrients 8, 9

O

otter 5
oxbow lake 15

P

peccary 22–23
pike 5, 8
piranha 22, 23, 24
pitcher plant 9
plants 8–9
polar bear 18–19
pollution 28
pond 8–9

R

reed houses 27
reindeer 19

S

silt 14, 15, 20
sitatunga 5
snakes 20, 22, 23, 25

T

tadpole 2, 16
tapir 23
terrapin 3
toad 7, 16
tourism 29
tundra 18–19
turtle 6

W

waterlily 4, 8, 30
willow 7